Floating Underwater © 2024 Ryan S. Hobbs

All rights reserved.

No part of this publication may be reproduced, stored in a retrieval system, or transmitted, in any form or by any means, electronic, mechanical, photocopying, recording or otherwise, without the prior written permission of the presenters.

Ryan S. Hobbs asserts the moral right to be identified as author of this work.

Presentation by *BookLeaf Publishing*

Web: www.bookleafpub.com

E-mail: info@bookleafpub.com

ISBN: 9789358319064

First edition 2024

Floating Underwater

Ryan S. Hobbs

BookLeaf Publishing

India | USA | UK

ACKNOWLEDGEMENT

I would like to thank everyone who has featured in my life, even for a fleeting moment. I also have some who I would like to mention by name...

Francesca Spencer, Tara Huzar, Nick Cox, Ffion Wilson-Wright, Gillian Flood, Lucy Hancock, Glen McWhinnie, Freyah McWhinnie, Lucy Hobbs, Tailia Parsons.

Tara Hobbs - being on the other side of the world does not mean your support is not valuable. It's needed and appreciated. Know that I'm always proud of you.

Mum and Dad - if I was born again and had an opportunity to choose my parents, I'd choose you both every single time.

Rafael Hayes, Verity Ashburn, Daniel Howell, Olivia Roe - Raf, Vee, Dan, Liv. My Mains. For everything and for it all. I shudder to think of what 2023 looked like without you in it.

Sunetta Wanjiku Kiarie - my heart, my love x

Grief

Grief is indiscriminate, don't care 'bout gender
nor 'bout age
Grief is searching for a reason why you're
feeling all this rage
Grief is all time standing still but somehow
you're still getting by
Grief is asking questions, never finding answers
as to why
Grief is doing things, not cuz you want to but
because you should
Grief is finding strength to do things that you
never thought you could
Grief is going back through every conversation
that you had
Grief's regret and pain for any time you were a
little mad
Grief is worrying that there are memories that
you'll forget
Grief is something gripping you, not letting up at
all nor let-
-ting you forgive yourself for any times you
raised your voice
Grief is forgetting that none of this was your
fucking choice

Grief is tryna find some sense in things that
aren't supposed to make it
Grief is finding ways to cope and believable
ways you can fake it
Grief is just a by-product of losing something
that you love
It can be comfort, wrapping itself round you like
a winter glove
Grief is panicked looking for the signs their
spirit's still around
And finding nothing, leading to your mental
health go through the ground
To rock bottom, tear-sodden, downtrodden,
All these feelings normal, all you want to do is
stop 'em
Grief will creep up on you in a moment when
you flash a smile
Grief will make you feel guilt, you can add that
to the growing pile
Grief will never leave you, build your life
around it then you'll see
One day you'll invite Grief in to join you for a
cup of tea
You'll find a way to live together, live like
neighbours, never friends
Grief will be there with you, watching over you
until your end

The Lady In The Rocking Chair

She spends her days in her rocking chair
Her eyes are vacant, she's losing hair
Years of wisdom are lines in her face
She's spent a really long time in this place

Intentionally slow, she rocks to and fro
She can no longer walk, and she has nowhere to
go
She does nothing alone, she gets cleaned, she
gets fed
All she has for herself are the thoughts in her
head

For her, talking means effort, therefore she
rarely speaks
When words form in her mouth, the world's
attention she piques
'I've lived a good life, and I'm happy,' we're told
'We all get to be young, some don't get to be old'

Letter To My Current Self

Dear me, dear you, I know it's hard for you to
wake
And you wonder how much more of this you're
just supposed to take
But it was unexpected. Don't you understand?
A year like this one never has formed part of the
plan
But look, it happened. And you adapted
You got here, to today, and to me, that's the mad
bit
Six months ago you couldn't see past the same
day
Couldn't see through to a time where all your
struggles go away
And you still don't, cuz they're not gone, they're
all still here
But as each day passes, so does your fear
You can get through this, because you're getting
through
All you have to do is believe the strength in you
And stop, giving yourself such a hard time
It's not going to help you further down the line
You're always told that you're so damn strong
And if everyone is saying it, it can't be wrong

You don't have to take on everything, no one's
thinking that but you
Sit back, take a look, and just choose the things
you do
Then press forward, work hard at them, find
yourself some faith
Remember, sometimes, winning is knowing that
you cannot win the race

If I'm Not Here, It's Not There

If I close my eyes, the consequences, I'll ignore them
A parallel world, my feelings, I'll explore them

meirl

Enter the room
No one I know
Turn back around
Through the door, home I go

Mostly I Live In A Morose State But Sometimes I Feel Like I Can Take On The World And Today Is One Of Those Days

Come for me
If you really want to
Why come alone?
Bring your whole crew
Me versus all of you
Opportunity to prove
That taking me on
The last stupid thing you'll do
There's no need
For you to arm me
I have the backing
Of the whole of Hobbs' Army
I won't be leaving
Are you barmy?
I'm not going anywhere
Yo quedarme
I'll gain notoriety
Win over society
Joyous crying in the streets

Mentally, between the sheets
I'm the leader of the world
Come together, love unfurled
Standing tall, whatever weather
Beat our fears, we'll be together

Guy On The Tube

Hey Guy on the Tube wearing one and a half
shoes
My name is Ryan, how do you do?
What's that you're eating? It's all over your hand
Oh, it's a box of coleslaw. It looks pretty bland
You seem to like it though, but, no fork or
spoon?
Just sitting, public transport, early afternoon
With some cabbage and mayo, shaping your
hand like a hook
You're on the phone talking and...goodness me,
look
You're tounging the box, every nook, every
crack
You're going for gold and you're not holding
back
And it's got more interesting, I've realised there's
no phone
With a mouthful of coleslaw, the words are
angered in tone
But I'm sorry Guy on the Tube, it's a language I
don't know
And looking at other travellers, it's the same for
them, so
Your words getting louder, I don't think will help

But you're unhappy with something, that's
something we felt
You're getting up now, it seems Faringdon's your
stop
You stand up, right your cap, straighten your top
You step off the carriage, and on with your day
Guy on the Tube, I hope you're okay

Ugh

There's a huge line in your head, right between
your eyebrows
And it's disgusting, but oops, too late for Botox
now
I look at you sometimes, and honestly, lord only
knows
How you keep yourself upright with the size of
that nose
And it's just the wrong shape, or maybe not the
right angle
Sitting on your face like a misplaced triangle
Brush your teeth more, they're going really
yellow
I won't take you seriously if you don't get them
whitened fellow
I first noticed that you had a sizeable belly when
you were eight
You were big boned, it had nothing to do with
any food you ate
But I know you've been self conscious about it
ever since then
Why can't you just get abs, like the rest of your
friends?
What about your feet? Look at them! What the
hell!

It looks like from each other they're just trying to
repel
When you walk it looks like you could topple at
any moment
Your back will pitch in, seize up, and for a
minute you are frozen
Don't drop your head, look at me when I'm
talking to you
Don't you know that if you look away, then
you're classified as rude?
It's not like you can see me really, I know to you
that I just blur
Okay, I'll stop, I know you hurt, I won't make it
any worse
Come back, we'll do this again, and maybe I'll
seem clearer, clearer
I fucking hate you, mess I see looking in the
mirror, mirror

Unknown

Take your chances
Don't wait
Follow your heart
Not your head
If I had listened to that
I would've said I love you one last time
It might have changed everything
It might have changed nothing
I'll never know

'God'

I don't believe in 'God', I don't think He exists
One of the more compelling arguments for this
Is how can 'He'? When there's so much hurt and
strife
How can 'He' arm a schoolchild with a knife
That ended up in Ellianne, she was protecting
her friend
That was enough for her young life to end
There's so much pain, there's so much war
There's a little bit of rich, but there's so much
poor
People fighting over which 'God' they choose to
believe in
If they choose the wrong one, well, they must be
heathens
Is that enough to justify committing genocide?
Is that proving your love to 'God', in 'His' eyes?
'God' doesn't care about me, I'm not a favourite
When it comes to religion, I don't think I'm
made for it
'He' took my girl, she was only twenty-nine
'God' and 'His' world all expect me to be fine
She was an angel, but 'He' took her for 'Himself'
So there's proof 'He' doesn't care about me, my
mental health

My future plans, everything we were working
for, together
In a four minute window, my whole life had
changed forever
'God' doesn't care about me, my wants, my needs
I refuse to give up, to be brought to my knees
But do you understand the pain of feeling
Rejected by something you don't even believe
in?

in:Rotation

A new silent passenger has put me on the shelf
Why do I continue to do this to myself?
I know this one is temporary, it'll disappear soon
With any luck I be able to salvage some of the
afternoon
I don't want to get out of bed
But I need some tablets for the pain in my head
Anxieties float on the surface like a sea of buoys
It's silent, but inside me there is so much noise
This passenger works with the others, making
them stronger
Making the suffering feel much longer
Anxiety, you're more nervous, depression, you're
more low
All day you pray and beg for this hangover to go
Wake the next day, they've finally gone away
I'm never drinking again you say
A few days later, you're out with your friends
Getting ready to go through this process again

Sunshine & Onions

Wake up with a smile on your face
Leap out of bed, excitable
Sing in the shower and bounce around your
home
Dance your way to work
Laugh, smile, encourage
Do great work, be the one people come to when
they need to be cheered up
Come home, quick change, go out
Social butterfly
Friends with everyone
Get to bed late at night
Fulfilled by a day well spent
This is how people think you live
To them, you are warm, glowing
You are sunshine

Wake up
Sad to have done so
Inner monologue trying to get you to get out of
bed
Sniffly, because your health never seems to be
perfect
Shower, mentally prepping for your day

Effectively living it before you actually have to
live it
Walk to work
Hope nobody notices you
Usually wearing sunglasses so no one can
properly see you
Recurring thoughts
What happens if you step into the road one
second too early?
Can't bring yourself to find out
Try your hardest at work but wish to be under
the radar
Though you never feel your work is good
enough
Be the one people come to when they need to be
cheered up
Easy to fake a smile if it's just for a few minutes
Exhausted after though
Come home, quick change, into clothes that
probably need a wash
Probably worn these for the last month of
evenings
TV is on, you're not watching, you just want a
little company
Food because you have to, but nothing that takes
more than ten minutes to get ready
Go to bed knowing tomorrow will be just the
same
The sunshine in you is tiny

This is the reality
Layer upon layer upon layer of unseen
You are an onion

Whine

Bottle of whine
Looking so fine
But I know if I drink you
I'll be losing time

Real

He doesn't want to lie to himself anymore
He sits down, sighs, wonders what it's all for
He's asked if he's okay. Yeah, I'm good
Stock answer, he answers how he thinks he
should

But what he really wants to say is

I can't deal with the news no more
Doom and gloom, hate and war
I'm struggling with what's happening in
Palestine, Israel
I missed Glasto tickets, have to rely on the resale
Why'd the media stop talking 'bout Grenfell
victims
How the fuck did Prince Andrew stay out of
prison?
Why'd my groceries cost more than they did last
week?
It's so expensive to be living, nah man, this is
peak
And it's sunny when I leave, rains before I arrive
All I want right now is just for warmth and to be
dry

Looked in the mirror this morning, need to
spend a month on salad
Don't feel that I can share my thoughts, my
opinions aren't valid
Everything is in my head and I feel so alone
I spend evenings in silence, sitting still, next to
my phone
Desperate for it to light up, to know that I'm on
someone's mind
To know that someone cares, but more often
than not, I seem to find
That it stays as dark as the space in my heart and
the tones that are in my head
Is this really living? Or am I already dead?

CV Of The Product Of A Dying Breed

SKILLS:

- Trustworthy
- Listening
- Compassion
- Respect
- Honour
- Some Kind Of Mental Illness
- Conversationalist
- Self Awareness
- Honesty
- Loyalty
- Integrity
- Empathy

Keeping On

How do we all keep carrying on?
On paper, I still have so long
The impact I've had on the world is less than
minimal
I've done so little, it feels so criminal
It's all so gloomy, I want to change it
Not only small stuff, I wanna change the main
shit
Politicians, war, murder, disease
Poverty so bad it's bringing momma to her knees
A world in which, if you're anything but white
You have a more difficult path in life
If you do the same job as a man
He'll earn more than you ever can
It's continuing, having gone on for so long
How do we all keep carrying on?

Impossible Expectations

I give myself a range and if those numbers come
back
I step off the scale thinking, yeah, I'm happy
with that
That's the theory, but it's far removed from the
reality
And all I achieve is that I just get mad at me
If I see a number, and it's within the range
I still walk away thinking 'bout what I need to
change
The thing about me - I'm never satisfied
If I tell you it's good, just know that I've lied
Strive for perfection, unreachable heights
Will I ever see my name go up in lights?

Yearning

27

You said it didn't seem to bother me
But I was hiding it, so
If I was hurting like you were
Then how would you know?

Just stay a little longer
Don't leave me just yet
One day we'll be laughing
One day we'll forget

I still believe that day will come
I'm counting down the time
'Til we walk off into sunset
Your hand wrapped up in mine

Nayeli

She would've been a good mum to you
You were our future, our happy place
Something that we looked forward to
Someone we looked forward to meeting
But we didn't get to do that
We didn't even try to create you
You were just a figment of our joint imagination
So now that she's gone
And the dream of you has died
I mourn her so deeply
And I mourn you too
Nayeli
Our beautiful baby girl

Can You Sit Down Please?

Can you sit down please?
My mind's already running
Full of possibilities, but I think I know what's
coming

Can you sit down please?
I'm stood frozen in time
Just a few weeks ago, I was hers, she was mine

Can you sit down please?
I haven't said yes or no
I say that I'm good standing, but to the couch my
body goes

Can you sit down please?
All these thoughts are racing through my head
What am I gonna do if I'm told that she is...
Can you sit down please?
The paramedic asks again
Nah, I think that she's okay.

I sit, and I'm sat next to, the medic takes a deep
breath, and then

'I'm sorry, but Sunetta has died'

In that moment, I wonder why, to myself, I have
lied

In that moment, a sound escapes me, I've never
heard it before
It's my soul, leaving my body, it can't take it
anymore

Physically I'm here
Mentally I'm with her

Dear Sunetta

Dear Sunetta,

You always like when I write my things in
rhyme,
So I'm here, writing to you for what might be the
last time,
We've known each other for nine whole years,
We shared so many laughs, and quite a few
tears,
A bucket load of memories, I'll share some here,
Most of them come from the last two years,
You moved in with me, and as quick as that,
You told everyone my property was YOUR flat!
I'd moved in for anonymity, to get away from
stress,
But suddenly the whole of Brighton seemed to
have my full address!
And the number to my phone! I was like what's
going on?!
But no one really knew that you felt you were
going wrong
You'd given me a call, told me some bad things
were happening
Asked me to come to Brighton, so I opened up a
map and if

I'm honest, which I was, I said I couldn't just
drop everything
But you could come and stay with me then any
bad stuff, we can bury it
You agreed and then arrived, a shadow of the
girl I knew
Worse than I'd imagined, I didn't know what I
could do
So I winged it, and I created for you 'Hobbs
Academy'
I made it a bit fun so that you couldn't be mad at
me
When I asked you to do some things you felt
you couldn't do
But you knew them necessary to be able to pull
through
Our days always started with Morning Hugs
Oh, Sunetta, what I'd give to give you one more
hug
And anyone you've hugged knows that they're
akin to GBH
You hugged so hard sometimes it felt my body
would break!
You worked so hard in those few months, I
really was the proudest
We found your laugh again, and as we know, it
was the loudest
You'd settled living with me, and you didn't want
to roam

So the title changed from my flat, or your flat, to
our home
You told me that you'd never felt as comfortable
as this
You'd walk around the place in your pyjamas,
hair bonnet,
Food stains on you and not a care in the world,
At your calmest, my beautiful, perfect girl
Maybe you didn't get better, but you found more
ways to cope
You kept telling me 'I'm trying' and kept trying
to find some hope
That Christmas I wrote you a song, to a
Hamilton track,
I took you to see it, we were sat at the back
When we were there, you sang the all of the
lyrics out so loud
That you were getting a few funny looks from
members of the crowd!
And our holiday to Spaignton, both so relaxed
and free
I took a video of you, walking out of the sea
And I showed you, and you cried, and you said 'I
can't believe
That the person in the video is actually me'
And there's a theme, because for all your beauty,
and love you were receiving
The demon in your mind was stopping you from
just believing

You never thought that you were capable of
being loved
But I loved you when you were here, and I'll
love you now you're above
And I'm grateful that I told you even if you
couldn't hear it
Words to describe how much probably won't get
nowhere near it
I want to thank you for holding on for these last
two years
And although I will continue to cry a huge
amount of tears
I'm so proud of you, for being you, for the
efforts that you made
I'll make sure the memories we have will never
ever fade
You helped me be the person, that I'm supposed
to be
I never told you that, and it's funny, cuz you see
You felt you couldn't be loved, but the line I said
right there
Was being saved, in case I needed it for our
wedding vows somewhere
I know it wasn't right for us right now to be
together
But I thought with us there would always be a
together, a forever
I said I'm writing to you for the last time, but
Suki I lied

Because physically you won't be here, but you'll
live on forever inside
You lit up my life, straight away, right from our
very start
You were my life, Sunetta, you were my entire
heart
Beautiful soul, to me, now and always, you'll be
perfect
You made these last two years of my life so
incredibly worth it
And so, you've finally found peace, and now
your mind can rest
I will never be angry at you if you thought this
for the best
You'll be starting on a journey so you can get
yourself some answers
And understand your feelings more my darling,
fellow cancer
And when you're ready, come and visit, come
and see me when I'm dreaming
I can't wait to see your massive smile, your
whole aura just beaming
You didn't believe when you were here, but I
was never lying,
You are my life, my heart, I love you very much,
love Ryan